Super Silly Riddles

CHARLES KELLER

**Illustrated by
Dave Winter**

Sterling Publishing Co., Inc.
New York

Library of Congress Cataloging-in-Publication Data

10   9   8   7   6   5   4   3   2   1

Published by Sterling Publishing Company, Inc.
387 Park Avenue South, New York, N.Y. 10016
© 2001 by Charles Keller
Distributed in Canada by Sterling Publishing
C/o Canadian Manda Group, One Atlantic Avenue, Suite 105
Toronto, Ontario, Canada M6K 3E7
Distributed in Great Britain and Europe by Chris Lloyd
463 Ashley Road, Parkstone, Poole, Dorset, BH14 0AX, England
Distributed in Australia by Capricorn Link (Australia) Pty Ltd.
P.O. Box 6651, Baulkham Hills, Business Centre,
NSW 2153, Australia

Sterling ISBN 0-8069-2791-7

Contents

1. Asleep at the Switch

What would you get if you crossed a camel with a cow?

A lumpy milkshake.

Where does a bull keep his business papers?
In his beef case.

What are the most religious animals?
Holy cows.

Why did the cow cross the street?
To get to the udder side.

What would you get if you crossed a birthday cake with an earthquake?
Crumbs.

Where does candy stay at a hotel?
In a suite.

What colorful letter can you eat?
A brown e.

What did Geronimo say when he jumped out of a plane?
"Me!"

What ailment do pilots experience?
Soars.

Do pilots get colds?
No, flew.

When don't airline employees wear uniforms?
When they are in plane clothes.

Why did the dolphin try to beach itself?
It had no porpoise in life.

What did the girl sea say to the boy sea when he asked for a date?
"Shore."

How do oceans make popcorn?
By microwave.

How does the ocean pay its water bill?
With sand dollars.

Water Dept.

How do baseball players keep in contact with friends?

They touch base with them.

What did the baseball glove say to the baseball?

"Catch you later."

Where do catchers eat their dinner?

At home plate.

Where is baseball mentioned in the Bible?

In the big inning.

Where do ghosts sit in the movies?

Dead center.

What does a baby ghost sit in?

A boo-ster chair.

What author works on Halloween?
A ghostwriter.

What would you get if you crossed a ghost with an owl?
A creature that frightens people and doesn't give a hoot.

Why do carpenters take so long to sign contracts?
They want to hammer out all the details first.

What do you call the female relatives of a house builder?
Carpenter ants.

Where do carpenters live?
In boarding houses.

Why do carpenters quit their jobs?
They get board.

Why did the bee join the rock band?
To be the lead stinger.

What do bees call their spouses?
"Honey."

How do buzzing insects talk to each other on a computer?
They use bee-mail.

9

What do you call a store owned by a bee?
A buzziness.

Which two dogs are opposites?
Hot dogs and chili dogs.

What do you call a pooch with too many ticks?
A watchdog.

What does a dog do that a person steps in ?
Pants.

If every dog has his day, what does a dog with a
broken tail have?
A weekend.

Why was Little Miss Muffet upset?
She didn't get her whey.

What's a hamburger's favorite fairy tale?
Hansel and Gristle.

In what factory does Humpty Dumpty work?
In an eggplant.

Why couldn't the three bears get back into their
house?
Because it had Goldie locks.

Why did the lion cross the road?
To get to the other pride.

What would you get if you crossed a lion and a porcupine?
Something you wouldn't want to sit next to on the bus.

Where do lions, tigers, and bears work out?
The jungle gym.

What do lions and tigers prey on?
Their knees.

Why doesn't a banana last long in a household?
Because a banana splits.

Do people like bananas?
Yes, a bunch.

What do you call a banana that has been stepped on?
A banana split.

What's green and goes a hundred miles an hour?
A frog in a blender.

What's a frog's favorite winter game?
Ice hoppy.

What do you call a frog stuck in the mud?
Unhoppy.

Where do you take a frog with poor eyesight?
To the hoptician.

Why did the shoes want to win the race so badly?
They couldn't accept defeat.

Why did the two shoes get along so well?
  They were soul mates.

What did the shoe say to the gum?
  "Stick with me and we'll go places."

Did you hear about the man who walked across
the country without shoes?
  It was quite a feat.

What do elephants wear on their legs?
  Elepants.

Why don't elephants play basketball?
They don't look good in shorts.

Why are elephant rides cheaper than pony rides?
Elephants work for peanuts.

Why do people eat chicken eggs and not elephant
eggs?
Because everyone hates elephant yolks.

2. Beating around the Bush

What did one hammer say to the other?
"I just broke a nail."

What did the waterfall say to the water fountain?
"You're just a little squirt."

What did one loom say to the other loom?
"Weave me alone."

Why is a new lawyer like an escaped convict?
They both passed their bars.

What do inmates do to amuse themselves in prison?
Sing Sing.

What's the hardest part of grammar for criminals?
The prison sentence.

When do you need to put football players and convicts on the same scale?
When you're weighing the pros and cons.

What animal is the first to rise in the morning?
The early bird.

Do birds memorize their flights?
No, they wing it.

What can you do to help a sick bird?
Get it tweeted.

How do birds get ready to exercise?
They do worm-ups.

What would you get if you crossed a computer
with an alligator?
A megabyte.

How does a computer eat?
Maybe a byte here and a byte there.

What animals help computers run?
Rams.

What was wrong with the cleaning lady's
computer?
It didn't do windows.

What's the best farm animal for boxing?
Duck!

Why didn't the duck pick up the restaurant check?
It already had a bill.

If a duck says "Quack, quack" when it walks, what does it say when it runs?
"Quick, quick."

What do you use to heal a broken duck?
Duck tape.

What egg is dangerous?
The eggsecutioner.

What's yellow and black and white?
Scrambled eggs with salt and pepper.

How does a beach like its eggs?
Sunny side up.

Why was the car embarrassed?
It had gas.

Why did the driver throw money on the street?
So he could stop on a dime.

Why did the battery cross the road?
It thought it would get a charge out of it.

What help should you seek after buying a rotten used car?
Lemonade.

How do vampires stay healthy?
They take bite-amins.

What do you call a dentist who offers to clean a werewolf's teeth?
Crazy.

What's Dracula's favorite dish?
The quiche of death.

Who do vampires prefer at the circus?
They go for the jugguler.

What do you get when you cross a fat football player with a pay phone?

A wide receiver.

How many football players does it take to change a lightbulb?

One, and ten others to recover the fumble.

How does a football coach go fishing?

With his tackle.

What's a couch potato's favorite sport?
  Channel surfing.

Why do sheep make bad drivers?
  They make too many ewe turns.

What do you call a lamb that fights on the ocean?
  A battlesheep.

How does a sheep protect its driver's license?
  It gets it lamb-inated.

What happens when you eat rotten bubble gum?
  You get gum disease.

What's a scientist's favorite candy?
  Experi-mints.

Why couldn't the girl keep Chicklets in her mouth?
  Because gum drops.

Why isn't it hard to protect children from cavities?
  It's like taking candy from a baby.

What game do ocean waves like to play?
  Pitch and toss.

What did the river say to the ocean?
"It's been nice running into you."

What do you call a teenager who cracks his
knuckles and swims in the ocean?
A salt-teen cracker.

What do surfers do when the tide goes out?
Wave goodbye.

What do you call a male bug that floats?
A buoyant.

What do call a female bug?
A gallant.

What did one lightning bug say to the other?
"Give me a push. I think my battery's dead."

What tree catches the most diseases?
The sycamore.

How does a tree change?
By turning over a new leaf.

What did the tree say when it couldn't solve the riddle?
"I'm stumped."

What are sleeping trees called?
Slumber.

Why was the violinist fired from the orchestra?
He was fiddling around.

Why was the violin so jittery?
It was high-strung.

What bows do violinists use to play their instruments?
Fiddle sticks.

3. Cracking Up

Where does Santa go swimming?
At the North Pool.

What use are skis and sleds?
Snow use.

Does it ever get cold in South America?
Yes, it can get quite Chile.

What kind of kitchen appliance is the Titanic famous for?
The sink.

What ice cream drinks weren't found on the Titanic?
Floats.

How did the escargot cross the ocean?
By snail boat.

Why do most ships sail the same routes?
Pier pressure.

What should you do if your ear rings?
Answer it.

How do ears keep fit?
With earobics.

What did the mitten say to the thumb?
"I glove you."

What kind of advice do you get from hands?
Finger tips.

How do rodents achieve their ambition?
They gopher it.

What is a rodent's favorite amusement park ride?
The ferret wheel.

What do rodents write on?
A mouse pad.

What does a doctor do with a sick zeppelin?
He tries to helium.

What doctor is famous for being lazy?
Dr. Doolittle.

Why did the leaf go the doctor?
It was a little green.

What do you call someone who treats sick ducks?
A ducktor.

How did the farmer find his daughter?
He tractor.

How did the farmer mend his pants?
With a cabbage patch.

Why did the farmer refuse to grow wheat?
It went against the grain.

Why isn't farm land expensive?
It's dirt cheap.

What works best when it has something in its eye?
A sewing needle.

How can you tell when a seamstress is going crazy?
She comes apart at the seams.

What's a seamstress's favorite piece of exercise equipment?
A thread mill.

How was the seamstress after the accident?
On the mend.

How did the pilot buy a present for his wife?
On the fly.

How did the busy track star do his homework?
On the run.

Why was the mortician fired?
He couldn't make his deadlines.

Why was the auto parts salesman fired?
He took too many brakes.

What would you get if you crossed a magician
with a snake?
Abra-ca-cobra!

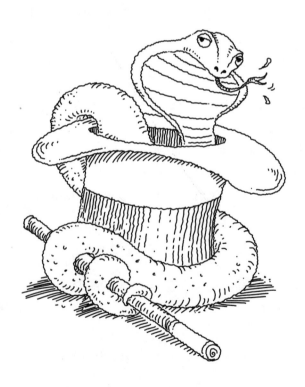

What would you get if you crossed pasta with a boa constrictor?

Spaghetti that winds itself around the fork.

Why did the snake keep checking the tires on his car?

He kept hearing a kind of hiss.

Why did the snake lose its lawsuit?

It didn't have a leg to stand on.

What's yellow on the outside and gray on the inside?

A school bus full of elephants.

Who gives money to elephants who lose a tooth?

The tusk fairy.

Why do elephants have cracks between their toes?

To carry their library cards.

What weighs twelve thousand pounds and is covered with lettuce and special sauce?

A Big MacElephant.

Why did the robber sleep under his bed?

He wanted to lie low.

What do you call a person who steals rubber bands?

A rubber bandit.

What's a thief's favorite metal?

Steel.

Why did the safecracker marry his girlfriend?

They were a good combination.

Why are birds so unhappy in the morning?

Because their little bills are all over dew.

What kind of hat does a bird wear?

A Robin hood.

Why did the bird ask the plastic surgeon for a new nose?
The old one didn't fit the bill.

Why do people feed birds?
For a lark.

What's a guitar player's favorite sport?
Bass ball.

What looks and acts like a male rock star?
A female rock star.

Why wasn't the musical group allowed to play?
They were band.

What's Batman's favorite way to swim?
Bat-stroke.

What's Superman's favorite street?
Lois Lane.

Who taught Superman to tell time?
Clock Kent.

4. Wits End

What does a tennis player use to start a fire?
Tennis matches.

What kind of money do tennis players earn?
Net pay.

What kind of students do letter carriers make?
First class.

What do students wear around their necks?
School ties.

What do class clowns snack on?
Wisecrackers.

What do high school graduates wipe their feet on?
Diploma mats.

Why do mummies like Christmas?
Because of all the wrappings.

What do you call a writer of horror films?
A screamwriter.

What did the papa monster say to his son?
"Father knows beast."

Who is the leader of the popcorn?
The kernel.

What should you say if a farmer wants to talk to you about corn?
"I'm all ears."

Why couldn't the paper doll walk?
It wasn't cut out for it.

Why did the gambler fight with weird people?
He wanted to beat the odds.

Why couldn't Tarzan call Jane?
Her vine was busy.

Why is Scotch Tape so successful?
It has a lot of stick-to-it-ness.

Why don't skiers get ahead in the world?
Because after they get to the top, it's all downhill.

What kind of horse collects stamps?
A hobby horse.

What office did the female horse run for?
Mare.

What has six legs, four eyes, and five ears?
A man riding a horse eating corn.

What should you do if your stallions start to gallop away?
Hold your horses.

What do you call a person who can't flip pancakes?
A flip flop.

What do breakfast eaters do on Saturday nights?
Cereal bowl.

How can you tell that a teapot is angry?
It blows its top.

Why couldn't the instant coffee sue the teapot?
It didn't have the grounds.

What famous fish wears a red, white, and blue hat?
Uncle Salmon.

What do you call a fish without an eye?
A fsh.

Who do fish get to clean their rooms?
  Mermaids.

What dessert do fish serve at parties?
  Crab cakes.

Why don't fish go away for the summer?
Because they are always in school.

If you really like coffee, what train do you take?
An espresso.

What trains carry bubble gum?
Chew chew trains.

Why did the railroad conductor return to his old job?
He wanted to get back on track.

What does a funny train ride on?
A laugh track.

What transportation do chefs prefer?
Gravy trains.

Why wasn't the crooked railroad conductor arrested?
Because he covered his tracks.

What is the laziest vegetable?
The couch potato.

Which vegetables have rhythm?
Beets.

What's a llama's favorite vegetable?
Llama beans.

What vegetable will listen to your problems?
Corn. It's always willing to lend an ear.

What award do they give to wonderful Grandmothers?
Grammies.

What is the smartest mountain?
Mt. Rushmore — it has four heads.

What's the best way to buy holes?
Wholesale.

What should smokers do to quit?
Butt out.

What piece of clothing do you put on an envelope?

Address.

What's worse than a giraffe with a sore throat?

An octopus with tennis elbow.

Why do giraffes make good friends?

They really stick their necks out for you.

Why didn't the bee have extra time?
It was always buzzy.

How do bees brush their hair?
With honeycombs.

If a bee married a rodent, what would its children be called?
Brats.

What language do bees use?
Buzz words.

What does a bee use to cut wood?
A buzz saw.

5. Gags to Riches

What do you call a jail that is specially designed
for baseball sluggers?
   The Grand Slammer.

What word is frowned at by baseball players but smiled at by bowlers?

"*Strike.*"

Why do most baseball games have to be played at night?

Because bats sleep during the daytime.

Why are tailors good talkers?

They know how to talk off the cuff.

What did the tailor do when his assistant arrived late for work?
He dressed him down.

Who sails the seven seas and makes good suits?
Sinbad the Tailor.

What's large, yellow, and lives in Scotland?
The Loch Ness canary.

What's yellow and goes "putt, putt, putt"?
A canary playing golf.

How do canaries earn extra money?
By babysitting for elephants on Saturday night.

Why can't Friday beat up Saturday?
Because Friday is a weak day.

What kind of shirt always needs a shower?
A sweatshirt.

What did they wear at the Boston Tea Party?
T-shirts.

What's the best shirt to wear into battle?
A tank top.

Why did the girl protest being expelled for wearing a tank top?
She wanted the right to bare arms.

What kind of dog washes clothes?
  A laundro-mutt.

What do you call the top of a dog house?
  The woof.

What part of a canine helps you find your place in books?
  Dog ear.

What did the boy say when his puppy ran away from home?
  "Doggone!"

What do you call someone who steals your puppy?
  "Doggone thief!"

Why do puppies eat frankfurters?
  Because it's a dog-eat-dog world.

Why do Wall Street investors take only showers?
  They don't want to take a bath in the market.

Why did the businessman buy a herd of cattle?
  His future was at steak.

How did the tailor do in the stock market?
  He lost his shirt.

What do you call it when a police officer quits?
Cop out.

What happened to Charlie Brown's girlfriend
when she got in trouble with the police?
*She was carted away in a Peppermint Paddy
wagon.*

What happened when a hundred hares got loose
on Main Street?
The police had to comb the area.

How should police officers deal with the public?
Uniformly.

What do you call a flower shop that's burning?
A florist fire.

Do some flowers ride bicycles?
Yes, rose pedals.

What flower believes in past lives?
Rein-carnation.

Why did the writer move from his ranch-style house?
He wanted more than one story.

What would you get if you put butter on your mattress?
A bed spread.

Where should you go to buy a comforter?
Downtown.

What chef thrives under stress?
A pressure cooker.

When does a chef know he's in trouble?
When his goose is cooked.

Why was the gossipy chef fired?
Because he dished out the dirt.

How do you know when a cat burglar has been at your house?
Your cat is missing.

Why was the clumsy cook fired?
She spilled the beans.

Why can you rely on the sun?
It always rises to the occasion.

What did the tree say when spring came?
"What a re-leaf!"

What did the summer say to the spring?
"Help! I'm going to fall."

How did King Kong escape from his cage?
He used a monkey wrench.

How did they train King Kong?
They hit him with a large rolled-up newspaper building.

How do you get a giant into a frying pan?
Use shortening.

Why did the blind man join the navy?
He wanted to go to see.

Why did the talkative man gain so much weight?
Because he liked to chew the fat.

Why did the reporter buy an ice cream cone?
He was desperate for a scoop.

Why did the river go on a diet?
It gained a few ponds.

Why did the rancher get mad when the thief
stole his hay?
  Because it was the last straw.

Why did the cowboy ride his horse to town?
  Because it was too heavy to carry.

Why did the cowboy go to the rodeo?
  Because wild horses couldn't keep him away.

Why did the cattle get upset when the rancher talked about eating beef?

They heard.

How do cattlemen plan for the future?

They make long-range plans.

6. April Fool

What would you get if you crossed a slob with an artist?

A messterpiece.

How do artists become famous?
It's the luck of the draw.

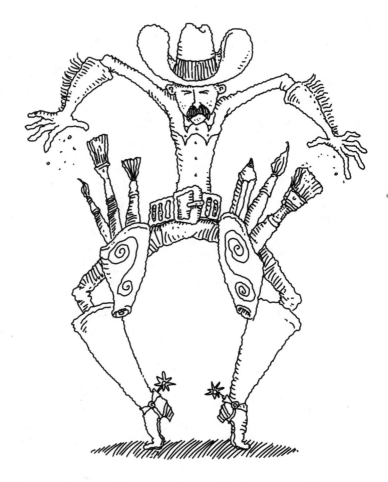

Where do gunslingers show their artwork?
At shooting galleries.

What kind of angel was Noah?
An ark angel.

Why did the angel go to the hospital?
She had harp failure.

Why do the windows in a house of worship have to be cleaned so often?
They're stained glass.

What would you get if you crossed a pig and a porcupine?
A stick in the mud.

What do you call pigs that drive trucks?
Squeals on wheels.

Why did the pig cross the road?
To get ink for his pen.

What do pigs do when they get angry?
They go hog wild.

What's big, lives near the beach, and wears sunglasses?
A two-hundred-pound seagull.

What do you call a beach that keeps losing sand?
A shore loser.

What was the tow truck doing at the racetrack?
Trying to pull a fast one.

Do truck drivers have tough jobs?
Yes, they have many bumps on the road.

Why did the truck driver's wife divorce him?
He drove her up the wall.

Why don't rabbits play football?
Their ears don't fit in the helmet.

How can you find out how big your skunk is?
Use a scent-imeter.

If a skunk wrote a book, what list would it be on?
The best-smeller list.

What animal is the least known?
Anonymouse.

What did the clock say at noon?
"Hands up."

What do you call an attack by a bunch of wigs?
A hair raid.

Do barbers like to dance?
No, they just like to cut in.

Was the man wearing his toupee in the wrong place?
Yes, they pulled the rug out from under him.

How does a wig introduce itself?
"Hair I am."

What do hairdressers do at the end of their lives?
They curl up and dye.

Why didn't the judge have any friends?
He held everyone in contempt.

What did the judge do with the hit-and-run driver?

He sent him to the prison baseball team.

What's a lawyer's favorite meal?

Brief Stroganoff.

When two bullets get married, what do they have?

BB's.

Why did the boulder's wife divorce him?

Because he took her for granite.

How did Benjamin Franklin's wife get rid of him?

She told him to go fly a kite.

Is it hard to be an IRS employee?

Yes, it's very taxing.

Why did the millionaire refuse to move to Alaska?

He didn't want to freeze his assets.

What animal can you borrow money from?

A loan wolf.

What do you call a small tick on the moon?

A moon buggy.

Where do aliens keep their teacups?
On flying saucers.

Why was there no more room for another
astronaut on the space shuttle?
They were outer space.

What would you get if you put a lightbulb in a suit of armor?

A knight light.

Can the king's son write longhand?

No, he prince.

What does the queen do when she gets mad at the king?

She crowns him.

Why did the king think that he could write a book?

He already had a title.

What did the flashlight say to the battery?

"You turn me on."

What's the most dangerous light?

Ultraviolent.

What kind of attention span does a light switch have?

On and off.

What color do nudists prefer?

Buff.

Why didn't the circle enjoy the dance?

It was a square dance.

Why was the inchworm angry?
It had to convert to the metric system.

What's the most disgusting unit of measurement?
Gross.

When is the best time to see a circle?
When it's around.

What unit of measurement likes to take charge?
A liter.

What do you call a yo-yo that doesn't come back up?
A yo.

What's a counterfeiter's favorite toy?
Play dough.

What are a writer's least favorite toys?
Writer's blocks.

Where do spies do their shopping?
At a snooper market.

What law do hitchhikers abide by?
The rule of thumb.

What book comes with its own light?
A matchbook.

What happened when the broom competed against the dustpan?

It was a clean sweep.

What is the rank of an Army dentist?

Drill sergeant.

7. Monkey Business

How do they play basketball in Hawaii?
With a hula hoop.

Why did the basketball player bring a suitcase to the game?
In case he travels.

What do stallions use to fly?
Horse feathers.

What do you call a pony that doesn't whinny?
A little horse.

What public opinion poll do horses like best?
The Gallop Poll.

Why didn't the bird make the curtain call?
He was waiting in the wings.

What did General Bird say to his army?
"Retweet! Retweet!"

What's convenient and weighs two tons?
An elephant six-pack.

Why don't elephants tip bellhops?
They like to carry their own trunks.

Why do elephants have trunks?
Because they can't carry all their stuff in their makeup case.

What would you get if you put 100 pounds of peanuts in an elephant's cage?

A happy elephant.

Why did the peanut butter jump into the ocean?

To be with the jellyfish.

Does margarine have wings?

No, but butterflies.

Why do most cities have the same stores?
It's a mall world.

Where does a lumberjack go to buy things?
To the chop-ing center.

Why did the actress go the bakery?
She was looking for good roles.

Did the actress stop dating the movie star?
Yes, he's out of the picture.

What do models eat off?
Fashion plates.

What do sound waves travel on?
The Earie Canal.

Where do you find bargains at sea?
On sale boats.

What's the most unpleasant boat to travel on?
A hardship.

How did the firefighter quit his job?
In the heat of the moment.

Why did the race car driver quit the circuit?
He wanted to shift gears.

How did the man's new job as a shoe salesman start?

He got off on the wrong foot.

Why didn't the plumber like his job?

He found it draining.

How did the laundry woman look after a day's work?

Washed out.

Where are great dragons remembered?

In the Hall of Flame.

How does a dentist fix a dragon's teeth?

With a fire drill.

What animals are the most computer literate?

Spiders. They practically live on the web.

What do you call it when spiders marry?

Holy weblock.

Why was the spider surprised by the doctor's bill?

It was charged an arm and a leg, an arm and a leg....

Are spiders a global problem?

Yes, as witnessed by the World Wide Web.

What creature helps repair computers?
Debug.

Where does a turtle go to eat out?
A slow-food restaurant.

What's green, sour, and weighs over five tons?
A picklesaurus.

What do you call a pickle that draws?
A dillustrator.

When do you go on red and stop on green?
When you're eating watermelon.

What would you get if you put a jar of honey outdoors overnight?
Honey-dew.

What did the man say to the grizzly?
"Bear with me."

What kind of bears enjoy lying in the sun?
Solar bears.

What's the difference between a buffalo and a bison?
You can wash your hands in a bison.

What do you call a llama's mother?
A mama llama.

Why did the banana go to the doctor?
It wasn't peeling well.

Why did the hog go to the eye doctor?
Because of his pig sty.

What illness is caused by the third letter of the alphabet?
C-sickness.

How did the doctor make money?
By ill-gotten gains.

8. Out on a Limb

Why did the talkative photographer take pictures of the steer?

He liked to shoot the bull.

What would you get if you crossed a cow with an octopus?

A farm animal that milks itself.

What would you get if you crossed a parrot with a pig?

A bird that hogs the conversation.

Why do leopards have spotted coats?

Because the tigers bought all the striped ones.

Why is it hard to find a store that will sell leopards coats?

No one wants to wait on them.

Where does a clerk put vile letters?

In the vile cabinet.

Why did the mall store owner bring bongos to the store?

To drum up business.

Why did the store manager hire the cow?

To beef up sales.

How long is a pair of shoes?

Two feet.

What did the zero say to the eight?

"Nice belt."

How do pants address mail to each other?
With zipper codes.

What do farmers do when they make money
selling pigs?
They live high on the hog.

Why couldn't they give the award-winning farmer his prize?
Because he was outstanding in his field.

What did the silly man name his pet zebra?
Spot.

Why did the nineteen kids go to the movies?
The sign out front said "UNDER EIGHTEEN NOT ADMITTED."

What did the mother rope say to her child?
"Don't be knotty."

Why wasn't the sportsman wearing clothes?
He was hunting bare.

What kind of bird hunt is never successful?
A wild goose chase.

What makes a goose different from other animals?
Most animals grow up, but a goose grows down.

Why do people get goose bumps?
Because camel bumps are too big.

What do factory workers and gardeners have in common?
They both do plant work.

What is the most foolish part of a tree?
  The sap.

What furniture is the most entertaining?
  Musical chairs.

What furniture is designed for those who like
seedy food and a swim outdoors?
  A birdbath.

Why is a leaking faucet like a racehorse?
  Because it's off and running.

What did the washer say to the drier?
  "Let's go for a spin."

What heating device should really go on a diet?
The potbelly stove.

What do you call a cafeteria after a food fight?
A mess hall.

What do you call someone else's cheese?
Nacho cheese.

Who won first prize at the beauty contest?
The winner.

Who was the biggest liar in the world?
The super duper.

What do you call a fly with no wings?
A walk.

What did the top fly do when the others didn't
do their work?
Fireflies.

How do you kill a fly?
Call in the S.W.A.T. team.

On what road do plants travel?
Routes.

Why do bagpipers walk so fast when they play?
To get away from the noise.

What comes after a tuba?
A three-ba.

Why must you be in good shape to become a singer?
You have to be able to carry a tune.

Why did the musical conductor bring the steer into the orchestra pit?
He wanted to take the bull by the horns.

Do singers tell you how they feel?
Only if it's off the record.

What city do sharks come from?
Shark-ago.

Why did the shark spit out the clown?
He tasted funny.

What do you call a whale that talks too much?
A blubber mouth.

What's the favorite dance of sardines?
The can-can.

What sea creature is the biggest celebrity?
  A starfish.

Why did the cat put its kittens into a drawer?
  It didn't want to leave its litter lying around.

What do hurt cats say?
  "Me-OWW!"

What's a cat's favorite dessert?
  Chocolate mouse.

How do you get milk from a cat?
  Steal its saucer.

9. Rib Ticklers

Why are fast-food restaurants so dangerous?
You might bump into a man eating chicken.

What do you call the wrong meat order at a restaurant?
A miss-steak.

What fat person brings you food in a restaurant?
A weightress.

What's the favorite subject at the South Pole?
Penguinship.

What do good students eat their burgers on?
Honor rolls.

Why did the teacher send the clock to the principal's office?
For tocking too much.

Why did the Fig Newton graduate first in his class?
He was one smart cookie.

How do card sharks walk?
They shuffle.

How does one amoeba talk to another amoeba?
On a cell phone.

Why wouldn't the customer buy fancy rollerblades?
He was a cheapskate.

Why did the customer refuse to buy a bed at first sight?
He wanted to sleep on it first.

Who is the biggest celebrity ever?
The sun. It's a superstar.

Why did the talk show hostess discuss forest fires?
It was a hot topic.

Why did the comedian quit his job?
He was at his wit's end.

Why are set designers difficult?
They make scenes.

What do you call a person with a loose wristwatch?
Someone with time on his hands.

How does a witch tell time?
With a witchwatch.

What happens when you eat crackers in bed?
You get a crumby night's sleep.

Where do campers snooze when they forget their sleeping bags?
On nap sacks.

Where do athletes like to stay?
In shape.

How can you keep cool at the ball park?
Sit by a fan.

How do hamburgers catch robbers?
With a burger alarm.

Where do you find silverware on a highway?
At the fork in the road.

What's a bat's least favorite hotel?
The cave-inn.

What luggage did the puppy bring on vacation?
A doggie bag.

What kind of luggage always makes a fuss?
Carry-on.

Why are some people afraid to go to the Big Apple?
They believe it's rotten to the core.

What do they use to clean clouds?
  A skyscraper.

How do successful weathermen get ahead?
  They take the world by storm.

What has five eyes and sleeps in a water bed?
  The Mississippi river.

What would you get if you crossed a monster
with a heavy rainstorm?
  A horrorcane.

Why were the bones chasing the skull?
  They wanted to get ahead.

What would you get if you threw Daffy Duck into
the Atlantic Ocean?
  Saltwater Daffy.

What did St. Nicholas build when he wanted a
place to put his clothes?
  A Santa Closet.

What flies through the air and is covered with
syrup?
  Peter Pancake.

What do you call a supernatural being with a
tan-colored rabbit?
  Genie with the light brown hare.

What's Tarzan's favorite Christmas song?
  "Jungle Bells."

Who is the Pied Piper's poor brother?
  The Pied Pauper.

Is it possible to lose your television clicker?
  It's a remote possibility.

How did the gymnast watch television?
  She flipped through the channels.

What's the most confusing part of the week?
  Week daze.

Why was the lumberjack so successful?
Don't ax.

Why couldn't the lumberjack keep up with his work?
He was backlogged.

What did the mental health worker carry instead of a briefcase?
A basket case.

What do you call polite butlers and maids?
Civil servants.

10. Tickled Pink

What are the chances of an artist making a living?

They're sketchy.

Why did the sculptor think he was going crazy?

He lost his marbles.

What happened when the artist threw a tantrum?

He showed his true colors.

Why don't foreign ambassadors get sick?

They have diplomatic immunity.

Where does the president of the birds live?

In the West Wing.

Which one of your teeth is always nice and polite?

Your sweet tooth.

Why did the guy use the daily paper for Kleenex?

He had a nose for news.

What part of your body is a real loser?

Defeat.

What kind of teeth can't be trusted?

False teeth.

What part of a letter carrier's anatomy is the first to go?

Deliver.

What's a computer's favorite snack?

Micro-chips.

What do you call brilliant Internet users?
Star tekkies.

What did the computer program and the itchy dog have in common?
They both had bugs.

Why did the computer hacker refuse to kill spiders?
Because he needed the web sites.

What do you call computer correspondence with a mouse?
Eeek-mail.

What do you say to speed up a turtle?
"Make it snappy."

What time do crocodiles meet their dates?
Date o'croc.

What cell phones do lizards use?
A repdial.

Why did the unhappy nun refuse to leave her job?
It's hard to quit the habit.

Why are mosquitoes religious?
First they sing over you and then they prey on you.

Why did the fish go to the priest?
Because confession is good for the sole.

Why did the fungi leave the party early?
Because there wasn't mushroom.

What's red and goes "putt, putt, putt?"
An outboard apple.

If an apple a day keeps the doctor away, what does an onion a day do?
It keeps everyone away.

What would you get if you crossed a water balloon with a needle?
Wet.

What would you get if you crossed a belt, a strawberry, and a shark?
Buckleberry Finn.

What's black and white and green?
A seasick zebra.

What's black and white and very dangerous?
A zebra on a skateboard.

Where do Arabs leave their camels when they go shopping?
In a camelot.

Are deer rebellious?
Yes, they always try to buck the system.

What do you call a near-collision of two dresses?
A clothes call.

What did the firefighter wear to work?
A blazer.

What crime was the celery arrested for?
Stalking.

Why did the bad check writer continue his crimes after jail?

He wanted to forge ahead.

What makes a loaf of bread happy?

Being kneaded.

What do bread bakers do on their day off?

Loaf.

What do geeks and nerds eat?

Square meals.

What side dish does a miner eat?

Coal slaw.

How can you give up cooking Thanksgiving dinner?

Go cold turkey.

What do people call chickens in prison?

Henmates.

Why was the hen so arrogant?

She had a large eggo.

What is a duck's favorite snack?

Quacker jacks.

What kind of test is the most irritating?

The cross examination.

Why did the school principal fire the lazy phys ed teacher?
   Because he didn't work out.

What should a teacher do when a deer gets an "A" on a test?
   Pass the buck.

How does a gym teacher travel?
   He flies coach.

What do you call two witches who live together?
   Broom mates.

How do witches break the sound barrier?
With a sonic broom.

Why was the baby ant so confused?
Because all of his uncles were ants.

What would you get if you crossed a robot with a skunk?
R 2 PU.

What do scientists do when they lose their keys?
Research.

What kind of weights do beginning bodybuilders use?
Paperweights.

What cup can't you drink from?
A hiccup.

What word has the most letters in it?
Mailbox.

Index